KT-132-419

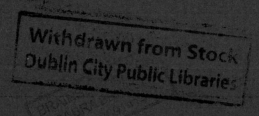

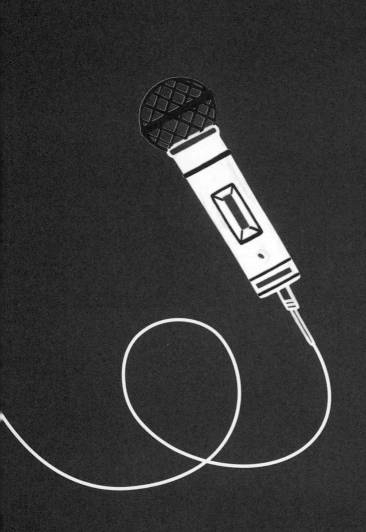

sing

Tune in to the
benefits of music
and find your voice

rosie dow

Illustrations by Jessica Meyrick

Hardie Grant

QUADRILLE

'If I
cannot fly,
let me sing.'

STEPHEN
SONDHEIM

CONTENTS

Introduction **6**

Why do we sing? **10**

What is music? **22**

What is singing? **42**

Couch to A5 **56**

Breaking barriers **104**

Your voice, your choice **120**

Quotes taken from **140**
Bibliography **140**
About the author **142**
Acknowledgements **143**

INTRODUCTION

To have a voice is to be human. Your voice is yours alone, a sound from the depths of your spirit, made from your body and imbued with your own unique story. In using our voice in song we share experiences and emotions. We connect with others and the world around us in a way that's unlike any other.

Singing confidently requires our bodies to be ready and our hearts and minds to be open. With a little knowledge and practice, I believe anyone can find their singing voice and, in doing so, can unlock the conviction and inspiration to share their story and transform their life for the better.

It's time to let the world hear your voice.

APPROACHING THIS BOOK

When was the last time you sang? Try it right now: open your mouth, breathe in and sing out. Sing anything: sing 'ooh', sing 'hello', or sing your name.

How did that feel? Perhaps you were a little nervous, or a little uncomfortable. Maybe your heart beat a little faster, or your voice sounded a little croaky and you felt you could have done a bit better. Perhaps it even felt like a small relief, as if you'd let something out that you'd been keeping inside. Or maybe you surprised yourself.

In that couple of seconds, whatever it was that you felt, you almost certainly felt something – something different from how you felt just before you started singing. Your body, your brain, your emotions all reacted. Something changed in you.

The aim of this book is to help you discover the potential of your voice – to continue that small transformation you just started and embark on a journey towards a more confident performance. My aim is to help you banish your fears and insecurities by giving you the information, tools and techniques to strengthen your singing voice and your confidence in it.

We will start by exploring the place and effects of singing in the human world, before exploring what music is, what the voice is and how it works. You will also hear from a few other people who've discovered a love of singing and whose stories will hopefully inspire you to persevere with your own journey.

We'll then move on to an accessible series of practical exercises that will provide a comprehensive and safe grounding in good singing technique. With time and practice, these will serve to improve your confidence, tone and pitch. We will also explore some common fears about singing and how to overcome those to really unlock your potential.

To get the most from this book, it's best to read all the sections fully, but if you prefer to jump around between the background information and the more practical exercises in the 'Couch to A5' chapter, that will work too. To help you put your new-found skill into practice and get the most out of your singing journey, the book concludes by looking at different styles and activities to guide you towards how to sing in your own way – to truly find your voice.

WHY DO WE SING?

Our desire to explore, explain and express our humanity is ongoing and never-ending. Both individually and collectively, we humans seek to discover, understand and share knowledge about the world around us.

Music and singing are both subjects of – and methods for – this exploration. A combination of the mathematical and the mystical, of the systematic and the enigmatic, singing is at the heart of our human quest for knowledge and expression. Listening to someone sing can affect us in a multitude of ways, inspiring delight or embarrassment, surprise or shock. But singing also affects us in diverse and powerful ways. So why do we do it?

'Singing is a way of escaping.
It's another world.
I'm no longer on earth.'

EDITH PIAF

TO CONNECT WITH OTHERS

Evolutionary anthropologists at Oxford University have likened group singing in humans to grooming behaviour among apes. Grooming triggers apes' bodies to release a hormone called oxytocin that causes them to feel bonded to each other. Mothers, both ape and human, also experience a release of this bonding hormone when they feed their young.

Because we humans have evolved to live more complex lives – and have less hair – than apes, some researchers say grooming is no longer a viable means of social bonding for us, so we have found different methods to connect us to other humans, such as speaking, laughing and singing. As well as a tool for the social bonding that is critical for our survival, singing communicates information, shows our prowess and expresses cultural identity. Group singing, which many millions of people do regularly, is tribal and powerful, a vital part of our human world of communication and connection.

CEIRIOS, SINGER
& SINGING TEACHER

I studied singing in college; now I teach and
sing solos. Musical theatre is my favourite,
because it means trying out different characters
while singing and getting to be someone else.
It's a different way of showing emotion.

I try to encourage others not to worry what
other people will think of their performance
and not to be too hard on themselves; this
approach has really helped me.

Find something that works for you. You may
prefer to be by yourself, or in a group. A choir
is a great thing to help build confidence and
meet other singers. Just go for it!

PETE,
CHOIR SINGER

I sing most days, to express an emotion and to relax. The combination of meaningful words and a good melody can really help a person understand their situation. Singing adds colour to a conversation. I find learning a new song very exciting, those first steps.

Listening to myself and to other people singing has really helped me, even if it was difficult at first. I now feel comfortable with my own voice and in a group. Whether it's in a choir, or belting out the last chorus at a favourite band's gig, that collective shiver from the shared experience is joyful.

TO EXPRESS OUR FEELINGS

But what exactly are we communicating when we sing? Are we just passing on information about water sources, fertile land, bus timetables, kings and queens...? To an extent, yes. But more importantly, songs tend to communicate something about our emotional response to our world.

We have several, innately primitive, vocal-like, bodily states that tell others how we are feeling. Crying, laughing, yawning: these are functions that we perform almost from birth, whereas we only learn to speak much later on. As we develop speech we also acquire certain inhibitions; societies, communities and families have various, complex conventions around how (and if) people should correctly express themselves. Speech and language can be hugely expressive of course; however, anthropologists have considered that singing operates in a sort of 'middle ground' between the sophisticated, but often restrained, function of speech and the earlier primitive sounds of emotional expression.

Songs contain elements of speech, in that they follow a structure and contain words, but creating the sound of singing also has physical similarities to laughing and crying, as we will explore later. Singing is both controlled and liberating; it therefore gives us a way of exploring and performing our feelings about the world in a structured way, so that we may find relief, develop empathy, build resilience and create mutual understanding in a safe and socially acceptable form.

There are numerous examples from around the world of how songs can help to safely express feelings. After spending time with the Kaluli tribes of Papua New Guinea, anthropologist Steven Feld wrote about how they expressed sadness through song, which he closely linked to weeping and birdsong. Meanwhile, Lila Abu-Lughod has written about how the structured song-poems composed and performed by the women of Bedouin tribes in Egypt provide a vital way of sharing feelings about their relationships and situations that social conventions prevent them from revealing elsewhere.

Singing allows us to communicate things that we can't always say, offering a less direct and more nuanced effect than simple speech. Ethnographer Carine Plancke describes a 'singing self', a sort of new self that we become when we sing. Inhabiting this singing entity allows us to express feelings we simply cannot when we talk.

TO FEEL BETTER

The link between songs and emotional communication means that singing can provide a release and relief from suffering. This is something we understand now better than ever: in recent years sociologists and biologists investigating the effects of singing have discovered a wide range of reported benefits, from feelings of euphoria (the 'endorphin rush'), to relaxation and stress relief, which they describe as both a psychological and a deeply physical response. Singers have described feeling less anxious and depressed after choir sessions, while soloists talk about the elation and sense of achievement they get from performing. Mothers who regularly attend singing sessions with their babies have reported feeling less worried and closer to their children as a result. Regular group singing has also been shown to build more powerful bonds, more quickly, between group members than other creative and social activities, leading to more cohesive workplaces, communities and societies.

JEAN,
CHOIR SINGER

I sing in a choir for people affected by cancer; I joined with my husband who has since passed away. Performing alongside him is one of my most treasured memories. The choir is my 'gig'; it holds me together now.

I think some sing to feel happy, others to relax. Perhaps everyone has a different reason for doing it. For me, it gives me a high, makes me feel less anxious and sad; it helps my grief. Time, practice and creeping confidence have helped me enjoy singing more and to improve – if ever so slowly at times. My favourite songs are the fun ones, the sentimental ones, and especially songs that mean something to me.

On an everyday level, singing is often seen as an enjoyable distraction from worries, boredom and even illnesses. A research study exploring the effects of choirs on cancer patients and their families showed that three months' of singing led to statistically significant improvements in their health-related quality of life, vitality and mental health, but it also alleviated some of their anxieties about their conditions and helped them to build a new identity after cancer, helping others to see them in a more positive and optimistic light. Folk singing is a particularly powerful form of advocacy: born out of suffering and tedium, the songs sung by slaves in America's Deep South not only lifted their spirits, but became a powerful emblem of their toil and turmoil, educating others about their plight. Singing told their story, and the world listened. Songs accompany, express and challenge our existence: the history of singing is the history of the world.

TO BE OURSELVES

Singing is deeply connected to our identities, both personal and cultural. Think of the national anthems sung at sports matches, which people join in with to feel part of a group whose members they don't know. Or think of a stadium full of rock music fans singing along to their favourite band. Soldiers' marching songs, cathedral choirs at Christmas, African songs at celebrations... they all tell both the singer and others who they are, uniting people and forming groups across great distances, if only for a moment. They're expressions of prowess and pride: we sing to show others who we are and where we belong.

But singing is also a deeply individual exploration and expression of our personal feelings and situation. Each of us has a unique anatomy, a unique larynx (voice box) and a unique story. As such, our voices are also exquisitely unique.

The relationship between humans and singing spans many stories and histories across the world. Singing has a unique meaning to each of us and yet bonds us all together in our humanity. It's a universal and vital activity that helps us to navigate the boundaries between ourselves and our collective existence, enabling us to build or maintain networks that are important to our enlightenment and survival.

SORIN,
LEAD SINGER IN A BAND

Since I was young I've loved singing. I sing to connect more closely with words and music that resonate with me and my experiences. I think we sing for expression, tradition, remembrance and connection.

When I was young I went through years of trying to emulate my heroes, but finally I learned how important it was to be happy with my natural voice. What really helped me was stabilising my internal resonance, I aim to be still – it's like a meditation for me.

My biggest challenge is still wanting to be able to sing every style, but I think it's important to sing for yourself, above all. Sing to make yourself happy, and if other people dig it on the way, just count that as a bonus.

WHAT IS MUSIC?

Music is many things to many people. It can partly be explained through a set of facts about sound waves and vibrations, but it also has many enigmatic quirks and effects we still can't fully articulate. Indeed, the effect music has on us is perhaps one of the deepest mysteries known to humankind.

Why not ask a few of your friends, neighbours or family members how they would define what music is, and how they feel when they engage in it? When you listen to their answers, focus on the subtle differences in their descriptions; think about the challenges they face in trying to articulate the precise nature and role of a system at once so simple yet so complex.

'Music produces a kind
of pleasure which human
nature cannot do without.'

CONFUCIUS

WHAT IS SOUND?

Sound is created when something vibrates. An object moves, or is struck, and this causes the air next to it to vibrate. These vibrations travel through the air, diminishing in frequency and volume the further they get from the original object until they hit our ears, themselves an intricate and complex system. Ears pick up the vibrations, which are then processed by our brains so that we get the sensation of 'hearing' something. Our ears are incredibly discerning: we can perceive hundreds of variations just in vowel and consonant sounds.

However, while anything can make a sound, that sound isn't necessarily music. If I picked up a set of random objects and bashed them together indiscriminately, I'd be making a noise but you probably wouldn't call it a tune. You wouldn't recognise the sounds as music, since they are not within a regular, familiar structure. Music is not just a series of sounds: it is a series of *organised* sounds – and much more, as we will come to discover.

MUSIC AS A HUMAN SYSTEM

Look around you. What sort of room or space are you in? Perhaps you are in your living room, or in a bedroom, study or garden. Wherever you are, it is likely that your surroundings will be pretty organised, with key identifiable features such as sofas, tables, beds or wardrobes. However, the precise design of your duvet cover, plants or pictures is much more likely to be personalised and individual to you. Together these common and individual aspects combine to make your house or garden work for you logistically, as well as to express yourself and your individuality.

We express ourselves by adding the unconventional to the conventional. There is a constancy and consistency to the underlying structures and systems in which we choose to live our lives, but within these we also crave distinctiveness and creativity. Much like the spaces we inhabit, music in its most elementary state is also a human system where structure and chaos combine in expression through a set of sounds that are at once regular and unexpected.

Within this organising, composers and singers place categorised sounds in different orders and at varying paces in an infinite number of sequences and combinations. So, just as the rooms in your house contain both constant, identifiable similarities to and clear differences from those of your neighbours, so it is with each piece of music.

The musical system comprises many dimensions, but in order for sounds to become music, they must generally have two things:

1. **An identifiable pitch**
2. **An identifiable rhythm**

From there, things get a little complicated, but bear with me: if you're going to embark on a singing journey, it's well worth knowing the basics about the system you're tapping into.

THE WESTERN MUSICAL SYSTEM

The descriptions here refer to the Western system of music categorisation, with respect to pitch and rhythm. There are other systems – all follow similar ways of categorising, but use different terminology. It's good to be aware that the Western system is only one way of describing music and is only used here to illustrate and explore the definition of music as a system of organised sounds.

PITCH

In music, pitch refers to how high or low a note sounds to us. In scientific terms pitch relates to the frequency of the vibrations caused by hitting or moving a certain object in a certain way: higher pitches oscillate faster than lower ones.

To create the musical system, universally agreed tones (notes) have then been given defined names. These follow the first seven letters of the modern English alphabet: A, B, C, D, E, F, G, moving up in pitch with each letter. If we start by playing or singing an A, moving one note higher is B, followed by C, and so on in sequence – D, E, F, G. After that G we then reach a 'top' A. We are back to an A because that A has twice the frequency of vibrations of the A note at the bottom. This mathematical occurrence would be true whichever note we start on, so a 'top' C is twice the frequency of the C eight notes below it. The gap between the top and bottom in this sequence of eight is known as an 'octave' ('oct' means eight, and the two are eight notes apart). Notes one octave apart sound to us as if they are the 'same' although the top one is higher than the bottom one.

SHARPS AND FLATS

This relatively straightforward seven-note system is slightly complicated by the addition of 'sharps' and 'flats'. If we think of the gap between each of the letters − A, B and so on − as a whole step between two notes, then the sharps and flats are midpoints, half steps, or what are known as 'semitones'. Sharp (#) means higher and flat (♭) means lower, so a C# is a semitone higher than a C, and a semitone lower than a D. C# is therefore also known as D flat (D♭).

This is true for five of the seven step 'gaps'; however ,just to add further complexity, there are two 'gaps' between notes that do *not* have a sharp/flat between them: these are the gaps between B and C, and E and F. This means there is no such thing as a B#/C♭ (or an E#/F♭), because B and C, and E and F, are already only one semitone apart. Again, this has to do with the frequencies of vibrations, and while it may seem a little confusing at first, it is something every musician eventually gets used to and accepts.

Thus in total there are 12 equal semitone steps in one octave, and 12 individually recognisable 'pitches' within the Western musical system, each step being a semitone apart.

ONE OCTAVE

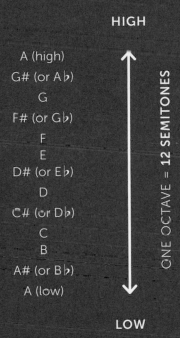

PIANO TIME

The easiest way to get a good grasp of the pitch system is with a keyboard or piano, which provides both a tactile and visual representation of the 12 steps, as well as the chance to hear the different pitches. Nowadays, you can even get smartphone piano apps – though nothing beats the real thing, of course.

A real piano is a string instrument. When you hit a key, a mechanism inside the piano causes a little hammer to hit a corresponding string, which creates the specific frequency of vibrations needed for that note.

Guitars – and in fact all instruments – work in broadly the same way, except that on a guitar we physically pluck the strings. On a wind instrument, it's the air travelling through a tube that causes the vibrations. However, it's the piano that is most helpful to beginners, because the keys are arranged sequentially relative to pitch; this is not always true of other instruments.

On a piano, each key refers to a different pitched note. Starting in the middle on, say, an A, the notes to the **right** of it are **higher** and go **up** the steps of 12 notes in sequence as you move key-by-key in that direction. Correspondingly, moving **left** gives you sequential **lower** tones.

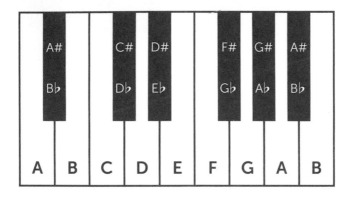

The black and white keys also help us understand the structure of the sharps and flats. White notes are the 'whole' notes (A, B, C, and so on – these are sometimes called 'naturals'), while black notes are the sharps/flats. You can see how they overlap – so G# is the same note as A♭, for example – and you can also see and hear that the B-C and E-F gaps have no sharps and flats between them.

Start by playing the low A white note and then move to the black A#/B♭ key immediately to its right. Notice how the half step up in pitch sounds. Keep moving up in half steps. Now try some 'whole' steps that have black keys between them, such as A to B, and listen carefully to the difference. Playing different combinations in sequence and getting your ear used to how the pitch moves up and down will be important for the singing exercises later.

It's how these different agreed tones – or notes – are arranged in sequences and chords that creates music. People may choose to arrange, organise or decorate them in infinite different ways to express different cultures, feelings, situations and personalities, but the underlying structure and system remains the same.

GET RHYTHM

Along with pitch, rhythm is the other vital concept in the musical system. It's not an easy thing to explain in words, but in simplest terms, we can understand rhythm as the length or duration of the notes in a piece or song and how they are played in relation to an underlying, regular pulse or beat.

Rhythm is about layers. At the basic layer each piece of music has a pulse, very much like a heartbeat, which can be counted in a repeated, regular way. When people say '1-2-3-4, 1-2-3-4,' over or under a piece of music, they are counting the basic beats in that piece. These can be fast or slow, but they are always a steady repeated pulse with equal 'gaps' between each beat. Some pieces are on repeating counts of 2, 3, 5 or even 6, but the basic idea remains the same.

In the next layers, you might hear several different rhythms, but all will 'fit' above that basic beat. Many varying rhythms are often played in one piece of music simultaneously – in backing vocals, on different instruments, and so on – adding richness and interest.

TRY IT

Put on a piece of music and listen to it to see if you can identify the pulse underneath. In a pop or rock song, this will often be played on drums and/or bass guitar. The vast majority of songs will be 'in 4', meaning they have an underlying count of 1-2-3-4, 1-2-3-4...

There are a few good examples 'in 3' as well, just so you can hear the difference. Songs with a very strong beat include:

Queen: 'Another One Bites the Dust'
(in 4, count of 1-2-3-4, 1-2-3-4)

Seal: 'Kiss from a Rose'
(in 3, count of 1-2-3, 1-2-3)

Pink Floyd: 'Money'
(in 7, count of 1-2-3-4-5-6-7)

EARWORMS

Why do certain songs or melodies seem to stick in our heads? Researchers across the world have used the earworm phenomenon to study music's effect on the brain. Some believe that certain elements of a melody may make some songs more 'singable' than others, and therefore more memorable and more likely to become an earworm. For example, having little gaps in the melody or fewer big jumps between low and high notes.

Studies have also found that we are more likely to remember and experience the earworm phenomenon with songs that we either sing along to or are sung to us, rather than purely instrumental pieces. This has led researchers to conclude that the voice is closely linked to memory and that we perhaps have early, pre-conscious memories of our mother singing when we were in the womb.

How these harmony and melody lines sit over the regular beat and interact with it (some notes may fall on the beat, some before, some after) is what gives a piece of music its character and often its style. For example, pop music melody rhythms often place the melody notes just before the beat for a driving effect, whereas classical music melodies are much more likely to coincide with the beat.

EXPECTATIONS VERSUS REALITY

Of course, the magical thing about music is not the fact that it's a system. That's just science and frequencies. What's special is *how* we travel between notes, and in what order and rhythm, which we do to *tell a story*.

Each melody line's particular journey – how we play or sing different notes in particular combinations at the same time – is fundamental to music. There are infinite combinations of notes and rhythms, but there are also common patterns that we recognise, and it's this blend of the expected and the unexpected in music that we seem to respond to on an emotional level.

Music is a learned system that has traits we all perceive – some combinations make us feel sad, others joyous, others nothing at all. But at the same time the instrument, the mode of performance and the style are all highly individual expressions chosen by one person or group to express particular ideas and tell a story, a story different from all other pieces of music. Music is science, but it is also art.

GOOSEBUMPS

Have you ever listened to a piece of music and had a physical reaction to it? Have the hairs stood up on your skin, or have you felt a sort of rush? Goosebumps result from a release of stress hormones that makes us more alert and causes the little muscles around our body hairs to react.

Scientists are not certain why they occur with music. Some theorise it's to do with the way it plays with our expectations. Our brains seek out patterns and repetition, which music gives us. But music also blends in the unexpected – changes in melody or rhythm that we aren't ready for. These can put our brain on 'alert'. Music can also evoke emotions, which themselves may cause a kind of stress – excitement or sadness, for example.

THE COLLECTIVE AND INDIVIDUAL EXPERIENCE

How many times have you loved a song that your sibling or friend dislikes? Have you ever met anyone who agrees 100 per cent with the contents of your music collection? The answer is most likely 'no', and yet 50,000 people can all share an experience such as a rock concert and feel joy and exhilaration as one. Music brings us together, but it can also defines and separates us.

In a concert hall the same vibrations from a violin, guitar or singer go out to every audience member. But each person there will hear and experience this in a slightly different way. This is partly physical, since our ears all have slightly different designs. But also our brain draws information from our individual set of life experiences, which will generate subtly different emotional responses from the same song. All audience members can agree that a concert features a particular set of notes played in a particular order, but it is virtually impossible that they will all experience the music in exactly the same way.

This is the magic of music – it is an organised, universal system of sounds, and yet it is also a beautifully complex and unique experience for each person engaging in that system. Past and present, physical and emotional, individual and collective, remembered and new, expectation and surprise – all merge into a momentary musical experience.

No wonder music is such a powerful thing. And in studying music we accept that while we can analyse and interpret the musical systems of notes and rhythms in diverse, rich and subtle ways, we may never fully unravel its mysticism. Therefore, in experiencing music through learning to sing we are engaging in something that is vital to our development as human beings, but at the same time, it is something we may never fully understand.

WHAT IS SINGING?

Singing is a musical sound produced by our voice system – the set of muscles and organs in our body that work together to produce noise.

The voice system is quite amazing, with many, many muscles and organs working together. This makes our singing voices incredibly varied and flexible – no other instrument can conquer anything like the range of styles and notes that our voices can. Better still, your voice is unique to you. We all share the same basic anatomy, but the exact shapes and sizes of our vocal systems make each of our voices different.

Understanding a bit about how the voice system works is a great basis for both improving and varying our singing ability. The more we know, the more we can do.

MAKING A SOUND: THE BASICS

Lighting a fire requires three things – fuel, heat and oxygen – producing a sound with our voices also requires three things to happen.

1.   AIR PRESSURE

Air is the fuel of the voice, which we acquire through breathing: taking air into our bodies (inhaling) and blowing it out again (exhaling). Each exhalation causes pressure changes within our lungs, throat, nose and mouth. We can consciously control the precise manner and speed of these changes by altering how we exhale.

Try to breathe out very quickly, or very slowly – you'll notice that your throat muscles react in different ways depending on how you exhale. This is important for singing, as it is our exhaling breath that creates the air pressure needed to make a sound.

We exhale using our lungs, the muscles between our ribs and underneath our lungs (our diaphragm), as well as our back and stomach muscles. Take a moment to think how much of the body creates the air pressure needed for us to make a sound. The vocal system is so much more than just our throat.

2. VIBRATION

Like the spark that ignites the fire, when we exert pressure on the voice box in our throat this causes vibrations. Even breathing normally will produce some kind of sound, but for this sound to be loud enough to be speech or singing we need far more significant vibrations. That's where our voice box (larynx), which houses our vocal folds, comes in.

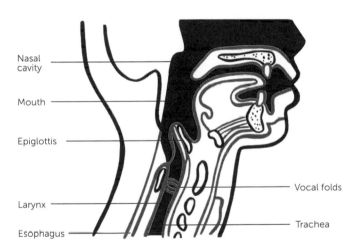

Nasal cavity

Mouth

Epiglottis

Larynx

Esophagus

Vocal folds

Trachea

Our vocal folds are two pieces of cartilage at the top of our trachea, or windpipe, that we can consciously open or close, by relaxing (opening) or tensing (closing). When we open our vocal folds, air passes through freely and quietly. But when we close them and exhale, the air pressure on them greatly increases and they start to vibrate very quickly. This intense vibration is the source of the sound we know as our voice.

Try just saying 'hello' and stopping after the 'he' part, freezing all your throat muscles where they are. You'll notice changes in your throat: a feeling of increased pressure and of closing or stopping the air just before the sound comes out.

When you look at the illustration (on page 45) you'll also notice how small your vocal folds are: about the size of your nostrils. Despite this, they are incredibly powerful. When we speak or sing they vibrate between 100 and

1,000 times a second. The quicker the vibration – which again we can control – the higher the pitch of the sound we make; this is how we sing 'higher' or 'lower'. The vocal folds are an amazing achievement of evolution when you consider what they can do, and have done, for humans.

Believe it or not, the voice box is not in a fixed place in your throat – it can move vertically, up and down your trachea (windpipe). This movement changes the quality of the voice, and can help us alter the amount of vibration and so the pitch of the note we're singing. You can feel this happening for yourself: place one of your fingers across your voice box; it's that bump on the front of your neck. Rest your finger there gently and then make a spoken 'ah' sound. Now, drop the pitch of that 'ah' so that it goes as low as possible. Can you feel your voice box move down and then up as you raise the pitch again?

3. RESONANCE (HEAT)

As heat is to fire, resonance is what creates the environment for the voice to succeed. Because our vocal folds are so small, the sound produced there is, in isolation, quite quiet. If we want our voice to be heard by others, it needs to be amplified.

To that end, we have our own remarkable internal amplification system, which consists of the cavities – or spaces – in our throat, mouth, nose, and whole head. Once our vocal folds produce a sound, it bounces around, echoes and resonates throughout our nose and mouth to be amplified, and altered, before it travels out to others through the vibrations in the air.

The precise design of our individual mouths and nasal cavities is what gives each of our voices its unique quality and tone. Although we can learn how to do voice impressions and accents – which again demonstrates the voice system's great agility and power – we all have a natural voice that is ours alone.

VOICE =
AIR PRESSURE +
VIBRATION +
RESONANCE

The voice has its origins in the depths of our lungs and stomach muscles, and is produced by vibrations in our throats that resonate or echo around our heads before leaving our bodies. Consider how intricate and beautifully designed the elements of your voice system are: they've evolved over millions of years to help you communicate, express yourself and build friendships. It'd be a shame not to use this all to good effect, don't you think?

It also follows that our whole breathing system needs to be in good shape and engaged in the right way in order for us to be able to sing well. Focusing on the voice box alone will not improve our singing.

MAKING A SONG

As well as the elements above, three more important ingredients are required for singing to happen – and to differentiate it from speech.

1. LISTENING

To be able to sing 'in tune' – that is, to fit the notes we sing to a system we know as music – we need to be precise in how we use our voices. Getting the specific vibrations of our vocal folds right so we can hit the correct pitch and move accurately between notes is only possible if we know what pitch we are aiming for.

Learning to sing therefore requires us to listen. Our goal is to reproduce a note or a melody line that we are hearing, and to do that we have to make a conscious connection between what we hear and the sound we make. Unlike repeating a section of speech, which can be done at any rhythm and any pitch, learning a song requires a lot more rigour.

Learning to listen is a skill. You can't expect your 'musical ear' to be tuned in immediately – you need to programme it. To do this, try tuning in to the pitch of things around you a little and often: the music in television adverts, on the radio, on a piano. Try humming at the same pitch as what you're hearing: are the notes the same? If not, do you need to move the pitch up or down?

There's a certain mysticism surrounding exactly how we reproduce pitch. We cannot consciously vibrate our vocal folds at, say, 400 times per second to produce a certain note (imagine moving your legs that quickly!). Vibrating our vocal folds also requires us to use the muscles around our voice box, not all of which we can fully feel. Nevertheless, something in our brain is able to process it all for us, and quickly. With just a little repetition and concentration, you'll find that once you start tuning in and listening to pitch and rhythm, it's remarkably easy to replicate what you hear. Then, all you need to do is work on strengthening your voice system to make those notes stronger, clearer and more expressive.

2. PRESENCE

Learning to sing requires us to engage our mind. After all, whether consciously or unconsciously, our brain controls our whole voice system. We are asking a lot of our bodies when we sing: we need to be able to manipulate some of our biggest muscles and organs (lungs, abdominal muscles) and some of the smallest (the vocal folds). This is impossible unless we concentrate on what we're doing.

Being present in the moment is one of the most important and beneficial aspects of singing. We should think of singing in a meditative way, only focusing as far ahead as the next note or phrase we're going to sing. Being able to fully connect and engage our minds and bodies in this way is a rare thing. In today's world we often live in relatively 'absent' ways – interacting with a range of people and stimuli through screens and across continents, thinking about the past and worrying about the future. So much so that some of us may be in danger of overloading our brains and underusing our bodies.

Not only does singing offer us a way to reconnect with ourselves, focus on the here and now and engage body and mind in perfect harmony, it *demands* it. All we need is a little guidance – everything else comes from within us.

3. EMOTION

In singing a song we are both reproducing and expressing deeply held feelings: joy, sadness, fear, pain, friendship. These feelings are what it means to be alive, which makes singing an expression of life in all its beauty and glory.

Many people find that when they start singing it brings up deeply held emotions. I have known lots of people to cry in their first choir sessions, and they can't fully explain why. Perhaps because music and songs are linked to our memories, both happy and difficult, and they remind us of the people in our lives with whom we have shared parts of our musical histories.

So simply making our vocal folds vibrate at the right pitches in the right order, with good support from our lungs and other organs, is never going to be enough to help us reach our full singing potential. In order for our voices to really make an impact, we must also learn how to connect with our fears as well as our happiness. This is a great blessing: most people who sing believe it is a huge comfort to have found a way to release their innermost emotions in such a safe and enjoyable way. In singing, we do not have to hide ourselves away.

'The total
person sings,
not just the
vocal cords.'

ESTHER BRONER

COUCH TO A5

'A5' is the note 'A' pitched at a high register. It's sometimes called a 'high A', and is more or less the top of the human singing range. With a few simple exercises, you can start your journey towards hitting that high note. It might seem daunting right now, and will almost certainly be difficult – many established singers find it so – but if you follow the right steps, you can get there, no matter how weak you think your voice is at the moment.

That means we're ready for the good bit: the singing! You know why we sing and the mechanisms that will underpin the learning process. Now it's time to put it into practice.

A NOTE ON PATIENCE – AND PRACTICE

Learning to sing well requires us to combine lots of different techniques and skills, making our brains and bodies work pretty hard. If you're right at the beginning of your journey, the following information might seem daunting at first.

My best advice is to work on just one or two things at a time. For example, this week or month you might choose to focus on connecting your breath to your diaphragm until you can do that without thinking too much. Then move on to your mouth shapes, or making sure your throat is nice and open. Think of all the exercises and techniques that follow as layers that you can add in at any time. Also have lots of breaks; it's best to work in short bursts and try to do a little each day; resting will help your brain to process the new information overnight and then you can try again tomorrow.

The most important thing is to find joy in what you're doing. Any song can be an exercise if you're working on one particular element, so if you choose music you enjoy right from the beginning, your performance will always be the better for it.

SINGING SAFELY

Singing can be an intense physical and mental activity. Over-using and over-stretching your delicate vocal folds, or not supporting your voice properly, could result in damage, so it's important to sing safely. This is also true of speaking: many teachers and television personalities experience damage to their voices through over-use. We are designed to speak and sing, but not all of the time.

Therefore, some top tips for keeping your voice healthy are:

1. **Hydration:** drink lots of water, especially before and during singing practice.

2. **Warm up:** do at least two warm-ups before singing a full song. The relaxation and lip bubbles exercises later in this chapter are particularly good for a quick warm-up.

3. **Hum:** always start with a hum; It's the gentlest sound on the voice box.

4. **Breathe:** always be thinking about your breathing. Is your diaphragm connected? Are you taking in enough air? Are you controlling that air pressure?

5. **Open your throat and mouth widely:** don't constrict anything.

6. **Take it easy:** there's no need to push your voice, a little can go a long way, and singing with a lovely soft voice can be much more effective than belting it out. Aim for a confident sound, not a pushed one.

7. **Rest often:** your voice will tire quickly when you are still learning. Don't push it.

8. **Stop if it hurts:** the vocal folds are delicate and can easily become inflamed or damaged. If you have any pain at all while singing, it's time to take a break. Also avoid singing during, or for a week or two after, any respiratory illness (cold or flu) or sore throat. If you're not sure, or have any long-term health conditions that have affected your throat, please check with your doctor for advice about singing and take it easy.

Before we can start singing well we need to learn to relax, correct our posture and breathe. It may seem strange to start a singing journey by not singing, but paying attention to your body is as important as the singing itself. Our bodies are our instruments and they need to be in the best possible condition; after all, you wouldn't expect a guitar to sound good if its strings were weak and its neck was wobbly.

RELAX

Tension is the enemy of good singing. When we are stressed, tired or worried about something, we carry those feelings into our posture, bones, muscles and organs. We tighten our muscles, we clam up and we do a lot of it unconsciously. What's more, because many of the muscles we need for singing are 'internal' ones that we cannot feel, we will not even be aware that they are tense.

Think of consciousness as a series of layers. Whatever we are thinking about at any given time – our focus – is happening at the top layer. Below that are all the peripheral or short- to medium-term 'projects' we are dealing with - we are walking, typing, watching, listening. We're also constantly taking in information, about our surroundings and our fellow humans. All this happens in the middle layers of consciousness. At the bottom layer, our brain is doing things we are far less aware of, such as breathing and regulating our body temperature, as well as holding much deeper-held fears. And all of this is connected. A fleeting worry at the top layer, a longer-term anxiety or grief in the middle layers, is directly linked to our muscles, breathing and energy levels at the bottom.

STRESSED OUT

Stress is a normal and natural human function, designed to warn us of danger and harm. When stressed our bodies release certain hormones – the chemicals that regulate our bodies and behaviour – that can temporarily energise or motivate us to run away or engage in conflict (this is often referred to as 'fight or flight'). They can also keep us alert for longer periods to deal with apparent danger. In small doses stress is useful for responding to threats or physical attacks. But if we feel it often, or for long periods of time, it can be bad for our mental and physical health.

Singing is a great way to relax. A 2016 study by Imperial College London and the Royal College of Music showed that, after an hour of singing, levels of the stress hormone cortisol in a group of choir singers' saliva had dropped significantly. This was also associated with better immune system function and lower inflammation markers. Amazing, isn't it?

To sing well, you need to be relaxed from the start. So how do you unwind quickly? Here are some simple exercises to help you physically and mentally de-stress and get rid of some of the physical tension you're most likely carrying. Beyond singing, they'll also help to relax you in any potentially stressful situation, from meeting new people to giving a presentation, or when you're just feeling a bit out of kilter.

NOTE: WE ALL HAVE OUR LIMITS

Only do as much of these exercises
as you're comfortable with, and feel able to do.

STRETCH

ARMS

Stand up, or sit up straight with uncrossed legs. Put down whatever you're holding (including this book – though obviously read the rest of this exercise first!). Then, check you're comfortable before reaching both your arms up to the ceiling. Keep your feet flat on the floor and your neck loose, ideally facing up towards your arms. Reach up high, and then let your arms flop by your sides. Repeat the exercise three times, breathing in as you reach up and exhaling as your arms flop back down.

DRINK IT UP

Hydration is as important to our singing muscles as it is for our general health. Vocal folds like to be wet and being well hydrated also helps to thin out mucus and keep our blood flowing – all good for budding singers! Good hydration is not as easy to achieve as you might think. Drink plain water, little and often, and increase your intake a little about 90 minutes before you start singing. Sipping honey in warm water may also help soothe the throat – and it tastes delicious! Finally, think about upping your intake of hydrating foods, such as fruit and vegetables. Of course, all these things are great for general health, too, and the healthier we are, the better we sing!

NECK & SHOULDERS

As humans evolved to stand up rather than crawl, our heads grew larger as our brains became more complex, and our backs, necks and shoulders took the brunt of the resulting pressure and tension. As a result, a good, careful stretch of the neck and shoulders can work wonders for releasing these muscles, which are clearly important for singing.

Place your hands on each side of your head (for support) and gently move your head sideways from one side to the other. You're not twisting here, you're just letting your head fall so that you feel a little stretch in the sides of the neck. Be careful to stop as soon as you feel the stretch, but hold it there a little to let the muscles relax. Repeat this a couple of times.

Now, place both hands, knitted together, flat on the back of your head and let your neck gently roll around. This should help you relax your shoulders, too. Finish off by rolling your shoulders around, with your arms relaxed by your sides. Try a forward motion and a backwards one. This one is like a little massage, and it's great for stopping you hunching and for easing tense muscles. Really enjoy letting go of all those stresses and strains. Relax. Breathe.

RIBS

This is a lovely exercise to do at home to release tension in all those muscles that join your ribcage together, which are also important for singing.

Sit on a dining room chair (not a sofa, armchair or office chair — it must be flat and unmoving) with both feet flat on the floor. Alternatively, kneel on the floor with both legs tucked underneath you. Place your arms across your chest, crossed over, so that your palms are touching the front of their respective opposite shoulders.

Now, gently rotate your whole upper body, including your head, towards one side, without moving your hips or neck at all – the rotation needs to come from your ribcage. At the end of each rotation you should be able to feel a nice gentle stretch in your ribs. Hold that stretch a bit before rotating to the other side. Do ten twists on each side, breathing in as you rotate and exhaling back to the centre. Then finish off with a few deep breaths.

Do this several times a day if you can; it'll really help strengthen and relax some of the key muscles used in singing.

FACE

Finally, place your hands on your cheeks and give your face a little massage, with your jaw nice and slack. Now, move your jaw around to try to release any remaining tension there. The jaw is one of the main places we carry stresses and strains, again often unconsciously.

Pay attention to what your tongue is doing right now. Where is it exactly in your mouth? If any of your tongue is touching the roof of your mouth, then your jaw and face are tense. Consciously peel your tongue away from the roof of your mouth and let it sit comfortably in the middle of your mouth.

PULL ON THE ROPE

This exercise really gets your blood pumping and helps loosen up your arms, shoulders and ribs all in one go!

Imagine there's a big rope hanging down from the ceiling in front of you – one of those thick ones used in, say, military training. Now, grab that invisible rope with both hands, just above head height, one hand just above the other. Start pulling it down, swapping your hands around when necessary, just as you would with a real rope. Keep on pulling for a nice, steady count of 20. Count out loud, too. This should get your heart rate up a little, as holding your arms above your head and moving requires your heart to pump blood 'uphill' to some big muscle groups. This makes it a great exercise all round!

'Those who wish to sing, always find a song.'

SWEDISH PROVERB

SHAKE IT OFF

The next thing you can do to get rid of tension is to shake out all your limbs. First, take your right arm. Breathing normally (don't hold your breath), shake the right arm eight times, above your head, as if you had just jumped out of a lake sopping wet and needed to dry off. Then repeat the process eight times with your left arm.

Now, shake your right leg out gently in front of you eight times (you may need to balance yourself by holding on to the back of a chair). Repeat with your left leg eight times. Repeat the cycle of shakes, this time to a count of four shakes per limb, then two, then one. This exercise is great because it relaxes your muscles, but also energises you.

Now, clasp your hands together in front of you at roughly shoulder height. Shake your hands (still clasped together) back and forth, so away from you and then back, for about 20 seconds. If you keep your jaw slack, this movement should also encourage you to shake your face, releasing any remaining tension.

YOUR MORNING COFFEE
(OR YOUR EVENING TIPPLE)

You may have heard that caffeine and alcohol can affect your ability to sing well. Scientists cannot seem to agree on whether coffee and tea are hydrating or dehydrating, so to be on the safe side it's best to be sensible and switch to drinking water or herbal tea after two to three cups of tea or coffee each day.

Coffee is known to contribute to acid reflux (heartburn) in some people. If this is the case for you, take care: reflux is linked to vocal fold damage. If you are worried about acid reflux or suffer from persistent hoarseness, coughing or sore throats, do check in with your doctor.

Alcohol, meanwhile, has been fairly conclusively proven to be dehydrating and should be avoided in advance of singing. Dairy (including in chocolate) also increases mucus production, which can inhibit good singing. Again, this may not be true for everyone; it's just useful to be aware that your diet and hydration plan needs thinking about if your voice is affected.

POSTURE

We don't just sing with our throat and mouth, but with our whole body. That's why it is important to pay attention to how we are standing when we sing (standing is always the preferred option for good singing).

FEET

First, look at your feet. Generally, we don't pay much attention to them, but our feet are our anchors, our support, our base. Their intricate design, the toes that allow us to be flexible, balance, move, walk, run – and to sing – are well worth taking a moment to marvel in.

For singing, your feet should be facing directly forwards, and running parallel to each other like train tracks. Avoid pointing them towards or away from each other. They should also be about hip distance apart.

NEED TO SIT?

If you are tired, less mobile, or simply sitting
for a while to sing in, say, a choir rehearsal, it's
still important to pay attention to your posture.
For singing while sat down, you should ideally
have both feet flat on the floor and be sitting
slightly forward on the chair, so that your back
is not fully against the back of the chair. Knees
and shoulders should be relaxed, and your
spine should be straight – imagine there's
a rope coming out of the top of your head
that's being pulled gently upwards.

KNEES & HIPS

Knees should be soft, and slightly bent. While you're stood up, with your feet well planted, roll your knees and hips around to make sure they are relaxed. You should feel slightly bouncy, ready for action, rather than rigid and confined.

Our hips are also important. As we humans have evolved to stand upright – which has opened up our lungs and enabled both speech and singing to develop – our pelvises have had to provide greater support for our rather fragile spines, necks and heads. So, check the position of your pelvis. Your bottom should be tucked in, not stuck out. Some of us need to readjust this when checking our posture as over time many of us learn to roll our pelvises back and out of position.

Having your feet well placed, your knees soft and your pelvis in the right position provides the best possible supporting space and structure for all the muscles around your lungs to work well when singing.

SHOULDERS

Finally, your shoulders. Again, we are aiming for a natural, neutral shoulder position. Many of us habitually hunch or slouch, meaning our shoulders are often higher and more forward than they should be. We often do it unconsciously as a result of lots of sitting, looking at screens, or even just wanting to be less conspicuous – this is especially true of taller people. Stress also contributes to hunching.

To realign your shoulders to lengthen out your neck, first consciously move your shoulders downwards. Then, imagine you have a little hook attached to the top of your head, and somebody pulls on that hook. This immediately straightens out the spine and aligns the shoulders.

Your posture should now be strong and ready for the next set of exercises. Just remember to remain relaxed. If you feel yourself getting a bit tense or uncomfortable, try shaking everything out and re-setting your posture by going through the same steps for feet, knees, hips and shoulders again.

Let's call this our singing posture. Take a moment to remember how it feels. Then, take a nice deep breath.

BREATHE

Breathing well is the single most important factor in singing safely and confidently. Breathing is the easiest and most natural thing in the world; it carries oxygen, our fuel, into our bloodstream and around our bodies. We breathe many millions of times in our lifetime, so however old you are, you will definitely have taken enough breaths to be pretty good at it.

So instinctive and basic is the act of breathing that we nearly always do it without thinking and that is perhaps our biggest challenge when it comes to learning how to sing. In order to sing well, we must learn to consciously use our breath in new ways.

Singing is one of the biggest and most strenuous applications of our breath that we can undertake, so we need to be prepared, with all the dimensions of our breath working well. There are many practices and activities that develop and support good breathing, including yoga, meditation and Pilates. Any of them will help you improve your breathing and strength for singing.

Whole books have been written about the art of breathing well, but for now, we will be approaching the subject through some easy exercises that are most relevant to singing however; there are a few fundamental things that we need to know about breathing and singing first.

BREATHING FOR SINGING IS NOT THE SAME AS BREATHING FOR SPEAKING

When we sing we use far more of our breath than when we speak. In learning to speak, we learn to economise on our breathing. Although it varies from person to person, humans tend to be chatty; speech is the glue that binds our societies, workplaces and families, so we simply wouldn't be able to spend so much time doing it if we weren't using as little breath as possible to do so. However, in order to sing well we have to ask much more of our lungs and of our whole bodies. If we sang as much as we spoke, we'd be exhausted and our voices would struggle. Being aware of this helps us understand how to apply our breath in the right ways.

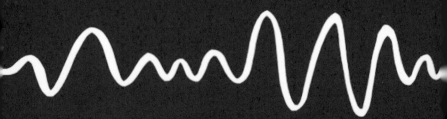

EVERY BREATH CAN BE FAR BIGGER

At rest, our breathing tends to be relatively shallow, so that we don't expend too much energy. We don't need to take in a lot of oxygen when we're relaxed, but if we walk up a hill or run around for a few minutes, our breathing rate increases and we become a lot more conscious of our breath. Our brains will soon tell us that we are tired and need to stop, again to conserve energy. This means we rarely use all of our lung capacity. For singing, however, we are aiming to breathe deeply and engage all our breath; we will soon be learning how much 'bigger' we can breathe.

WE CAN'T FEEL ALL THE MUSCLES
WE NEED TO USE FOR SINGING

Take a slow, deep breath. Repeat this a few times. As you breathe, think about all the parts of your body that you can feel moving. Not just your chest, but your stomach, hips, legs and arms are all probably engaged, too, as are all the dozens of internal muscles that surround your ribs, back and upper chest. That's before you even engage your voice box! However, it's important to realise that while there are many muscles you can feel moving, there are also many that you can't, especially in your throat.

So, how do you train muscles you can't feel? Unfortunately, there is no easy way – you just have to choose the right exercises and practise consistently. Doing so will establish the habits of good breathing and eventually your muscles will remember what to do, even if you can't feel them.

Many of the exercises that follow are aimed at rewiring your brain and body to breathe more deeply in preparation for singing, to use more breath, and not to economise on your technique. These can provide many benefits beyond helping you sing well. Breathing deeply and richly, often, is good for you; it helps you to relax and is a great thing to do if you are feeling a little anxious or wired, or having trouble sleeping.

CIRCLE OF BREATH

You should think of your breath as one continuous, repeating cycle. Slowly draw a circle in the air in front of you with one hand, roughly from your nose to your hips. Repeat this, and when your hand is at the lowest part of the circle, start inhaling until you reach the top of the circle, then exhale as your hand travels through the downward part of the circle back to your hips. Do not hold your breath between the inhale and the exhale, and try to exhale fully so that all your breath is out by the time you reach the lowest part of the circle with your hand. Repeat a few times. Don't you feel calmer already?

FIND YOUR DIAPHRAGM

In your singing posture position, place both hands on your belly, around where your belly button is. This is near the bottom of your diaphragm, the big internal muscle that supports the bottom of your lungs (and one of the muscles you can't really feel). Knit your fingers slightly together, so your fingertips are interlinked.

Continue the inhale-exhale circle, without the hand movements this time. As you breathe in, your hands should separate as your stomach expands. This is caused by your diaphragm expanding, which in turn forces your abdominal muscles to expand.

Now, on each of your out-breaths, make a 'shh' sound. This will accentuate the feeling in your tummy of expansion and contraction, as well as being extremely calming. Continue each 'shh' until the very end of your breath. This is like an internal stretch, since we rarely exhale fully before inhaling again. Just as you need to stretch before exercising, you need to warm up your voice muscles before singing, and the 'shh' exercise is great for that.

As you cycle through inhaling and exhaling on a 'shh' (do this ten to fifteen times), notice how large your breath is. Visualise all the areas of your body your breath is going into. Notice how much stronger and calmer you feel already.

EXPAND YOUR BREATH

Now you know that you have much more breath than you think you do, you can always improve your lung capacity – and it's really simple to do. A little practice every day goes a long way, and not only stretches your lungs but also helps control your breath better, so you can sing longer phrases, or more powerful shorter ones, entirely as you wish.

All you need to do is breathe in – a nice deep but controlled breath. Take your time and don't gasp, then breathe out on a 'shh'. Repeat, but this time, see if you can make the 'shh' last a little longer, say for a count of ten; use a stopwatch if you have one. After, try a count of fifteen. Every time you do it, try and make the 'shh' last a little longer. Thirty seconds is a good amount of time to aim for. It takes a lot of control to hold your breath back while exhaling in this way; it may seem difficult at first, but over time you'll get there and your lung capacity and breath control will improve tremendously.

This is something professional singers do all the time and some can reach 60 seconds or more. While that may seem totally unachievable to you right now, remember the only difference between you and them, in this respect, is practice.

ENGAGING YOUR DIAPHRAGM: PRIMITIVE SOUNDS

With your hands still placed on your tummy (see page 85), take a deep breath and exhale on a crisp 'ha!' sound. Make it an exclamation! Now, start laughing – this may feel a little odd, but don't worry about it being a genuine laugh, just focus on what's happening to your stomach and your hands as you laugh through 'ha, ha, ha!'.

No doubt your diaphragm is bouncing around and you can feel lots of movement in all your stomach muscles. That's because making a 'ha' sound forces you to engage your full set of singing muscles (our diaphragm, intercostal and vocal muscles – all those 'can't feel' internal ones). Some other sounds you can try are 'fff-fff' and, once again, 'shh-shh'.

Laughing or crying naturally engages our whole vocal system – any parent will tell you how powerful these sounds are coming from their babies compared to speech. Once we learn to speak, we laugh and cry much less, and of course we economise our breathing when we talk. We thus lose these good diaphragmatic habits a little as we grow up. Rediscovering them now means returning to our most basic expressive sounds to unlock great singing technique.

Performed regularly over time, these exercises help reconnect our diaphragm with our voice, giving us a more powerful instrument to sing with. When singing we're always aiming for our whole bodies to feel as connected to our breath as it does when we're laughing or crying. At first this might seem difficult, but keep consciously practising these exercises and it will happen.

HUM

The safest and most comfortable way to start singing is by humming. Even as you become more experienced, it's still a good idea to warm up by doing this. That's because full singing forces quite a lot of pressure from our open mouths down to our delicate voice boxes, whereas humming keeps our mouths closed, lowering the pressure on our vocal muscles.

Get into your singing posture and engage your diaphragm. Now, pick a note, any note, and start humming it. If you have a piano, play a C and try humming that. Visualise the sound coming up from your hips, through your whole chest and neck, and being placed just in front of your mouth. If you do this correctly, your lips should feel as though they're buzzing. Keep trying until you feel that buzz.

LIP BUBBLES –
THE MAGIC WARM-UP!

Just as picking up a heavy weight exerts pressure on our backs, so singing exerts pressure on our voice boxes.

The relationship between strong legs and weaker backs in weightlifting is a bit like that of strong diaphragms to weaker throats in singing. Because humans have such thin spines, weightlifters build up their leg and core muscles to help their backs withstand the pressure of raising weights. In singing, connecting our diaphragm to our breath is vital for supporting the voice box while under the pressure of singing. This, of course, takes time, as, like the legs of weightlifters, those muscles need to be built up, too.

A brilliant exercise that helps develop the throat muscles while neutralising the pressure on them is the 'lip bubble'. Flare out your lips and blow air through on a 'hrrrr' sound, while vibrating your lips very quickly; your tongue should be loose and vibrating in your mouth. The sound is a little like a horse 'neighing'. See if you can put a tone into the sound so that you are 'bubbling' and singing at the same time. Try moving the pitch of the tone around so that it goes higher or lower. This exercise is a little hard to describe in words alone but if you have a look online there are videos describing 'lip trills' or 'lip bubbles'.

'Lip bubbles' are a fantastic way of safely and comfortably exercising your vocal folds. I always recommend performing a few lip bubbles before singing to warm up the muscles and give your voice a little workout. Doing a little, often, goes a long way. Many professional singing teachers say this is the only warm-up they now use.

VOWEL SOUNDS

Now let's ease into some vowel sounds by adding an 'ah' to the end of our 'mmm'. We are aiming for a long note: play a C on a piano and try to copy it, starting with 'mmm' and then moving, without stopping, to 'ah' – 'mmm-aah'. See if you can keep the quality of the tone consistent and smooth, not forgetting to keep your diaphragm and breath connected. There's a lot to think about, but you can do it!

From the C, repeat the 'mmm-ahh' on the D note above it, moving up note by note until you can go no higher. Then move back down to the C and continue past it to go as low as you can.

Repeat the exercise on all the vowel sounds as follows:

mmm-ay

mmm-eee

mmm-aye (this sounds very much like mmm-aah but with an extra 'ee' on the end)

mmm-oh

mmm-ooh

Now, repeat all these but instead of the 'mmm' try a 'ha, ha!', so 'ha-ha!-aah', and so on. This acts as a check for your diaphragm – is it connected right through to your vowel sounds?

OPEN YOUR MOUTH

Now we are properly singing. As a result, the shape of our mouth suddenly becomes important.

As the notes resonate around our mouth and facial cavities, they need space in order to sound clear, powerful and in tune. That means opening your mouth.

When we speak we often minimise our mouth movements, but in singing we should aim to over-articulate, especially on vowels, which are more important to the quality of our singing tone than consonants.

You'll be amazed how much better doing this makes your singing – instantly!

VOCAL SIRENS

Now that your 'ooh' is sounding crisp, clear and confident, you might like to try some vocal sirens. These are great for extending your range, helping you to sing higher and lower notes than you can at the moment.

Sing any note that feels comfortable to you on an 'ooh'. Sustain the note, breathing and coming back in when you need to. Now, continue singing that 'ooh', but move down to the lowest possible note you can sing and stay there a moment, before sliding back up to where you started. Once you've done that, repeat the exercise, but go up to the top note you can sing and then come back down again. Your top note might be much higher than you think – open that throat and see what you can do (though stop if anything feels painful or uncomfortable).

Vocal sirens are powerful exercises that work all the parts of your voice safely, strengthening and stretching your vocal folds (and indeed your whole voice system) to increase your range.

SCALES AND ARPEGGIOS

In order to sing in tune our voices need to hit the pitches of the 12 notes in the music system precisely, and move smoothly and correctly between them. Broadly, the change between two notes can happen in two ways:

1. **Separate: where you move in a step change from one note to the next.**

2. **Slur: where the notes are joined and you slide from one to the other.**

Using your piano keyboard, start at the note C and sing 'laa', then move one note up and sing another 'laa' at that pitch. Continue up through each note until you reach the next C, then come back down again.

This is a scale. Start by practising scales where all the notes are separate and you move in step changes, then move on to the slurred version. Try the following sounds: doo, daa, mee, maa, lo, day. Aim for precision and clarity in each note, and in the transition – it's not as easy as it sounds (especially on the way down) and will require practise. However, over time this will really strengthen all your vowel sounds as well as your transitions, which is great preparation for songs and will make you a much more flexible singer, as well as expanding that all-important range. Remember, we're aiming for that A5!

Now, we can try jumping between different notes. Sing the following ascending notes in sequence on a 'laa': C, E, G, C, and descend back down on the same notes. Now try a semitone higher (so C#, F, G# and C#), and so on. This pattern is known as an 'arpeggio'. Try them both as step changes and slurred, again working through the different vowel sounds: doo, daa, mee, maa, lo, day.

Practising these scales and jumps will strengthen your voice and train your ears to keep in tune, as well as increasing your range and flexibility.

TONGUE TWISTERS

Now, repeat the C scale and the jumping exercise, but instead of singing 'laa', try singing the following tongue twisters:

- **Purple lorry, yellow lorry**

- **Seth at Sainsbury's sells thick socks**

- **Unique New York**

- **Comedy, comedy, comedy, comedy**

Sing the whole phrase, syllable by syllable, in C, then move up to sing it all in D, and so on. All the notes can be the same length, so don't worry about the rhythm, but try to sing them in a regular beat so they sound musical.

Tricky aren't they? Tongue twisters like these require the larynx to do a huge amount of moving around to get the right vowel and consonant sounds in the right order. They're like a circuit class for your voice. If you can sing these quickly – see how fast you can go – you can build a great platform for being able to sing almost anything.

SONGS TO TRY

So far, what you've learned are the basic tools and techniques you need to sing safely and clearly. Now, it's finally time to apply those to singing some songs!

Broadly speaking, there's no right or wrong choice when it comes to what songs to sing. If you're motivated to try something, go for it! Your singing will be most successful if what you sing is familiar and means something to you. That said, at the beginning of your journey you may wish to aim for songs that:

- Do not go too high or too low for you – though do continue to challenge yourself over time on this.

- Do not have big jumps in pitch, or very fast rhythms – though again you can work towards this as you improve.

Music shops sell lots of songbooks that are tailored to beginners, intermediate learners and so on, and there are guides online to this. You can also find lots of 'karaoke' videos online to sing along with, which is a great way to practise alone. Remember to keep thinking about your singing posture and technique while practising songs, even if you only focus on one technique at a time. You may therefore find that some of your Celine Dion favourites are best left until you're feeling super confident and you've worked on the top end of your voice through lots of sirens and lip bubbles.

That said, you'll only improve if you challenge yourself, so by all means give it a go — just remember to retain good posture and technique.

In the 'Your voice, your choice' chapter, we'll look at different styles of singing that use a range of approaches and mechanisms, as well as options for taking your singing journey forward so you can get the best possible enjoyment and satisfaction from it.

'HEAD' AND 'CHEST' VOICE

Have you ever heard the terms 'head voice' and 'chest voice' in relation to singing? Or have you ever noticed that when singing higher pitches your voice feels as though it breaks, and feels and sounds a bit different when you sing above a certain pitch?

Some people refer to the higher part of their singing voice as their 'head voice' and the lower part of their singing voice as their 'chest voice'. The terms are not necessarily scientifically accurate – they simply refer to the sensation of the high (head) and low (chest) registers in your voice, rather than where the sound is produced. In reality, our voice can only come from one place: the voice system, and specifically the vocal folds.

The vocal folds vibrate to make sound and can do this in subtly different ways, some more open, relaxed or stretched than others. That's what creates the different qualities between 'head' and 'chest' voices, or upper and lower registers. For higher notes in our upper register (head voice), the vocal folds are a little more open than for lower ones (chest voice). We can control this process consciously, although above certain pitches most people find that their voices automatically 'break' into their upper register to protect themselves from additional pressure.

Some vocal coaches believe we use the muscles at the back of our throats to control our chest voices, and the muscles at the front of our throats to control our head voices. The 'head voice' mucles tend to be more flexible, allowing us to sing faster or more complicated melody lines. Singing higher notes with our chest voices requires a lot of pressure and a very closed sound, which means a lot of energy and power, so many of us will find this rather difficult at first.

People often find that, especially as a beginner lower notes in the chest voice feel more comfortable than higher notes in the head voice, as the sensation is a little more like speaking and the 'break' can feel unsettling. But don't be afraid of those higher registers, as they can unlock a lot of flexibility in your voice and greatly expand your range so you can really hit those high notes, not to mention helping you to sing in a much bigger variety of styles.

BEWARE THE BELT

Singing high notes in a chest voice, or a mix of head and chest voices, is often known as 'belting' a note. This technique is common in musical theatre and pop singing.

Those new to singing who would love to belt out pop songs like Celine Dion or Jon Bon Jovi will want to train themselves up on this. But take care not to force your muscles – vocal folds are fragile and can be easily damaged if pushed too hard. Getting there will take a lot of practice and strengthening, and having the right support for your voice from the diaphragm is also important in belting to avoid damage. Many famous singers have damaged their voices through overuse of 'belting' and have had to have surgery. Always warm up, stay hydrated and keep your throat open – and if it ever hurts while you're singing, stop and take a break.

OPEN YOUR THROAT

To allow the right support to come up from the diaphragm to the voice, and to get a lovely clear tone, we need to open up our throats. Releasing tension in your body is an important step to achieving this (see earlier in the chapter for some great stress-relieving exercises). But you should also work on opening your throat while singing.

First, yawn. Then yawn again, and this time pay attention to how the yawn feels in your throat; it should be lovely and open. That's the feeling we're aiming for while singing. Now, pick any exercise – one of the tongue twisters is perfect. Try to adjust your singing so that your throat is as open as it was for that yawn.

Another good way to encourage the throat to open up is to hold your nose while singing. You may struggle with some of the consonants, but holding your nose shouldn't make any real difference to your vowel sounds.

BREAKING BARRIERS

As you went through the exercises in the previous chapter, it's likely you won't have always had the confidence you'd have liked to in your singing and you probably made mistakes. It's important to be kind to yourself and to find ways to overcome your self-doubts.

Being armed with a few insights into why people lack confidence in singing can really help to break through those doubts and be kind to yourself.

'A song can be more than words and music… when sung with soul a song carries you to another world, to a place where no matter how much pain you feel, you are never alone.'

CLAY AIKEN

'I CAN'T SING'

The self-limiting belief that a person can't sing (or, we may say, can't sing well) is extremely common, even among those who regularly sing. Other phrases with the same subtext include: 'I only sing when nobody's listening', 'I only sing in the car' or 'I'm tone deaf'. We may often laugh at ourselves when making these kind of statements, but while this might momentarily help us feel more comfortable about expressing our perceived inadequacy, it only reinforces the underlying message we're telling ourselves: that we can't do something.

Going through life repeating such phrases can instil ways of thinking about our capability that can prevent us from enjoying singing to the full. In order to fully get the most from our singing journeys, we need to train our brains to think positively about the learning process, and about our own abilities as singers.

There are a number of ways of doing this, but a little knowledge goes a long way in reframing the negative ideas and getting started in an optimistic way.

THINKING,
THEN FEELING

Have you ever heard the phrase 'Fake it till you make it'? Well, that's not exactly the approach we're taking here, but the sentiment does follow a useful pattern. The idea is that if you tell yourself to think a certain way, eventually you'll start feeling that way of thinking is true, even if you're not sure at the beginning. We can apply this concept to a few facts about singing in order to start reprogramming our thoughts and feelings about how we go about it.

WHAT ABOUT
ARETHA FRANKLIN
AND MARIAH CAREY?

It's true that certain physical traits in the voice box, lungs or oral and nasal cavities may make one singer 'sound' better than another. Singing stars may often have unusual anatomical setups that mean they tune in to music and find singing naturally a little easier. Again, this is no different to running: Olympic marathon runners likely have particular anatomies that enable them to run 26 miles more quickly than other people.

But at the same time there are many people who can run marathons or sing on stage extremely well who do not have such anatomical advantages. What's more, famous singers would not have achieved their success without also dedicating themselves to training and maintaining their vocal muscles to be the best they could be. Talent offers a beginning, but success comes from applying yourself.

Like any exercise, singing can be strenuous and even damaging if you are not careful. Some people suffer injuries or conditions that leave them unable to sing, just as others suffer problems that stop them from running. Poor technique risks your voice, so if you ever have any pain or discomfort while singing, stop and rest. If the discomfort persists, check in with your doctor.

THE VOCAL MARATHON

Think of the voice as a muscle – or more specifically, a set of muscles. Like any other muscle group, the voice can be weak or strong, depending on how you use it, how you train it, how often, and for how long.

If you wanted to run a marathon but had never gone for a run, you wouldn't expect to be able to simply get up from your couch, put on some trainers, and breezily jog 26 miles without stopping – or without seriously hurting yourself.

Singing is no different. To be able to sing confidently and safely for extended periods you need to invest time, exercise and effort in order to develop a good singing tone and build up the stamina of your voice. Musical theatre singers, who perform for hours each day, spend years training in order to build up the right strength to avoid damaging their voices. This may seem daunting at first, but seeing the exercises in the previous chapter as the key to unlocking your vocal 'fitness' will give you excellent building blocks from which to start your training.

COMPARING OURSELVES TO OTHERS

Today's pervasive celebrity and social media culture encourages us to idolise, or compare ourselves to, vocal perfection. Television talent contests have inspired many to take up singing as a hobby, but they've also given us a much more critical ear, and we're now harder on ourselves than ever when it comes to letting others hear us sing. After all, how could we ever match up to the latest talent contest winner?

But by appreciating the anatomical reality of our voices, we soon see that comparisons are fruitless. Our precise anatomies and spirits are wholly our own. Understanding that your voice is the action of a group of muscles, directed by your brain via your ears and combined with your spirit, you realise that your voice is unique – and that's the best thing about it.

VOICE =
MUSCLES + BRAIN +
EARS + SPIRIT

BEING TONE DEAF

Tone deafness is a rare condition that renders some people incapable of distinguishing the pitch of sounds or hearing that two notes are different. Scientists estimate that only around two to four per cent of the population truly suffers from the problem, compared to around 17 to 20 per cent of people who describe themselves as 'tone deaf'.

Therefore, only around one in ten people who say they are tone deaf actually are. This means that the other nine of that ten are perfectly capable of learning how to sing in tune; you are much more likely to be one of those. It's also worth keeping in mind that tone deafness is a problem with the ears and brain, not with the actual voice.

So what's going on with the nine out of ten people who think they're tone deaf but aren't? Well, remember the vocal marathon, and remember that we said voice = muscles + brain + ears + spirit. If you're singing the wrong notes, sound out of tune, or others tell you your notes are incorrect, what is most likely happening is that you haven't yet learned to connect your ears, brain and voice muscles, because doing so takes practice and skill. You're hearing the notes you're supposed to sing, but you haven't yet developed the right muscle memory in your vocal muscles to match the pitch accurately. Simply put, you need to do two things: listen and practise. The exercises in the previous chapter will help you overcome this. The first step, though, is knowing that you can.

HOW CAN I TELL IF I'M
TONE DEAF OR NOT?

The statistics show that you're probably not
tone deaf. But if you really want to be sure, try
this quick and simple exercise. You will need
either a piano, keyboard, guitar or ukulele
– you don't need to know how to play it.

If using a piano or keyboard, choose three
different keys, anywhere on the keyboard, and
play each one in turn, a couple of times. If
using a guitar or ukulele, pluck three different
strings. Do the notes sound different from each
other to you? Can you tell that some notes
sound 'higher' or 'lower' than others?

If the answer is yes, and you can hear
a difference, you are not tone deaf.

If the answer is no, and you can't hear a difference, try again several times. If you really can't distinguish the pitch of the different notes, only then is it possible that you may be tone deaf. Even then, don't give up! Many believe that pitch recognition can be improved by training the ear and brain to recognise pitch differences. Suggested methods for doing this include learning to play an instrument and booking a visit with an audiologist, as well as learning to sing (so no excuses!).

There are also a number of online tests you can take that will 'diagnose' whether you're tone deaf or not by playing you bits of music and quizzing you on what you hear.

OVERCOME YOUR EMBARRASSMENT

The feeling of embarrassment is linked to the fear of making mistakes, but is compounded by worrying about what other people think of us. Caring about others' opinions is a deep, lifelong instinct that applies to most of us in most situations. But while certain self-development enthusiasts might encourage us to ignore what people think – and you certainly shouldn't take unfair criticism or bullying to heart – completely separating ourselves off from others' views of us is impossible and may even be unhelpful. A bit of healthy concern for people's opinions is a survival instinct: forming strong social bonds is key to our thriving as a species, so we need to think well of each other.

Although we can't please everyone, all of us ultimately aim to please someone. Again, accepting embarrassment as a natural feeling is half the battle in helping us to better cope with it. The best approach is to ask yourself whether someone's opinion of you and your singing will be that affected by the odd wrong note, a weaker tone or a missed lyric? Perhaps if a professional singer made lots of mistakes during a concert that you'd paid to see, you might feel dissatisfied. But you can't apply that logic to your own singing journey as an amateur.

Even if the 'worst' happened and somebody did make a negative comment, it's worth considering whether you are singing for their approval, or to learn a new skill and enjoy yourself? It's much more likely to be the latter, and this motivation is key to overcoming any sort of embarrassment. This, and knowing that you're safe from dissatisfied customers for at least some time yet.

BE PATIENT

Many of us are perfectionist and self-critical, especially when we're learning something new. This can create impatience and the worry that we will 'never get it'.

Again, the way to overcome this is to remind ourselves that this feeling is expected and natural; it is a crucial stage in the learning process. Without putting a little pressure on ourselves, few of us would be capable of persisting with anything new. Of course, such pressure should never feel upsetting or be too prolonged, but we can definitely expect momentary frustrations as we learn to sing. Indeed, these are often signs that we are getting better, since we've come to expect more of ourselves.

THE LEARNING PROCESS: THE FOUR STAGES OF COMPETENCE AND CONSCIOUSNESS

Learning is a complex human process, not a linear journey. As such there are many theories about how we learn, and the different stages and feelings we go through when doing something new. It's not is an exact science, but a model developed by management coach Martin Broadwell in the 1960s, which is still applied by many business trainers today, may provide us with a bit of self-reflection and comfort on our singing journeys.

Broadwell's model suggests that we go through four distinct stages when we learn something. At each stage our ability to do something, our competence, crosses over with our awareness of our ability, our consciousness. All four stages directly impact our confidence and motivation in different ways.

1. **Unconscious incompetence** – when we first approach a new task, we largely feel excited although we lack real knowledge of what we are letting ourselves in for. We don't yet know what there is to know about the subject. We are unconscious of our own incompetence.

2. Conscious incompetence – as we begin to gain knowledge about a subject or activity, we start to appreciate and understand the things we don't know how to do yet. We know what we are supposed to be doing, but can't yet do it. We are therefore conscious of our own incompetence. This is often where frustration and demotivation can occur.

3. Conscious competence – after time, practice and effort, we begin to see and accept that we now know how to do the thing we are learning. But we still have to think about it, and often this means we don't yet feel fully confident. We are conscious of our competence, but we are still a little unsure.

4. Unconscious competence – eventually, as we practise more and more and get into the habits of our new skill, we start to be able to do it without thinking so much about it. This is especially true of physical activities, as our muscles have memories. If we consciously and repeatedly tell our muscles what to do, they will remember later on. We can be unconsciously competent, and feel great about it!

Seeing these stages as inevitable and anticipating them will help us to accept and overcome the associated difficult feelings when they arise. We will get there!

SEE MISTAKES AS PROGRESS

See and hear each wobble as an opportunity to learn and get better. What happened with that note? Did you forget to support it properly, or did you not take the time to warm up fully? Perhaps it was in a part of your voice you know is slightly weaker, and you need to go back to the exercises (lip bubbles work wonders on those little breaks and cracks between notes).

Nowadays, it's easy to record yourself on a computer or smartphone – most have a recording function and decent microphone. Remember, our voices sound different to ourselves from how they sound to others, so listening back to yourself is an incredibly worthwhile exercise, even if it's a little daunting at first. If you can get used to the sound of your voice, this will also help you to forget your embarrassment and use your recordings to really improve. You'll most likely end up surprising yourself with your progress and how good you sound.

Be sure to listen back to your recordings as soon as possible. That way you can remember what you were doing at the points that sounded good (and not so good). Then you know what to keep doing, and what to work on. You're sure to find that some techniques come to you more easily than others. The aim is to develop a well-rounded approach so that you always keep improving.

BE BRAVE

Fear of failing, of not being able to do something we want to do, is one of the biggest inhibitors to progress. It's also a self-fulfilling prophecy: if we're scared of failing, we don't try, and so we inevitably never succeed. Our fears are thus confirmed and multiply.

Now is the time to break that negative cycle and be brave. We have already established that with the right mental and physical approach, singing is a totally safe and enjoyable activity and there is nothing to be afraid of. We also know that we will make mistakes and experience frustrations, and these can be taken as positive signs that we are developing. None of this will stop your less rational anxieties from creeping in, but accepting setbacks as a natural and inevitable part of the learning process is the best way to move past them. Even if you do get the odd unhelpful comment from your nearest and dearest, you can counteract its effect by reminding yourself of your bravery. Be kind to yourself: tell yourself that you want to sing, for your own enjoyment and fulfilment, to communicate with others, or even just with yourself. Ask your friends and family to support you. Then, just do it. You'll soon learn that there's nothing to fear – and so much to gain.

YOUR VOICE, YOUR CHOICE

So far, we've focused on the building blocks of finding and strengthening your singing voice, with exercises and techniques to help you feel more confident as a performer.

But to what end? This is perhaps the most important question: what do you want to do with your singing voice, now that you've found it?

Your voice is yours, so it's up to you what you do with it. As you approach trying out the different styles and activities in this chapter, always remember to analyse and reflect on how singing makes you feel. You are singing for you, so seek enjoyment in the focus, challenge and progress singing offers, and in the proven benefits to your confidence, health and wellbeing. Give yourself credit for investing this time in self-improvement, creativity and enlightenment. It's the very least you deserve.

FIND YOUR STYLE

There are countless singing styles across the world. In this chapter, the focus is more on Western traditions of singing, but be aware that every nation has many more styles and opportunities than those listed here. Also remember that styles influence each other, so a musical theatre piece might include elements of soul, pop, jazz or folk – or vice versa. Composers and songwriters love to play with our expectations by challenging definitions of style. That said, there are some basic principles related to singing in different styles that can be useful to bear in mind as you choose which is right for you.

It's also good to remember the impact that fashions and cultures have on what we perceive as 'good' singing. Today's pop singers apply very different techniques, and so sound very different, from the jazz and classical singers who were the darlings of the 1920s. This goes to show that we don't need to always aspire to, or compare ourselves to, in-vogue singers as there is no universal, or timeless, definition of 'good' singing. Simply aim to sing in tune, with a strong tone – that's the substance of capability. The rest is just style, and perception.

CLASSICAL/OPERA

Professional classical singers work for years to train and develop their voices, which can make classical singing seem a bit daunting. But it can in fact be one of the more accessible styles of singing. It generally uses more of our 'head voice' (see p100–101), which is a bit gentler on the throat, has a bigger range and is more flexible.

The rhythms also tend to be much more regular and 'on the beat' than other more modern styles – lots of early composers approached their pieces in a mathematical way; this can make it easier on the ears and voice. If we try, most of us can imitate a classical sound quite easily by engaging our head voice, as well as by dropping our voice boxes to the bottom of our throats. Try it! You probably already do it automatically if you sing Christmas carols, anthems or hymns.

Classical singing remains popular, despite the fact that much of the music is hundreds of years old. Many community choirs and choral societies focus solely on singing in this style, and there are even choirs that only sing works by one composer, such as Bach, Mozart or Beethoven.

Delving into the world of classical music can introduce you to a whole community of like-minded people, performance opportunities and chances to develop your musical knowledge.

Opera singing tends to be more musically demanding than other classical styles, with more notes sung, in a bigger range and in more complicated and quicker rhythms. There's also a strong dramatic performance element. If you're interested in singing opera, it might be a good idea to find a vocal coach who can help you.

FOLK

Folk music is all about telling stories. These can be everyday stories of love and loss, or epic tales of fair maidens, tragedies and heroic journeys. Irish and British folk music is usually performed by bands using guitars and other string instruments, such as violins. In other countries the definition of folk music is broad: it is anything 'of the people'. Historically in Europe this meant non-religious music, since hymns and classical works were generally commissioned by the Church or government. In contrast, folk music had its origins in the fields and farms of the peasantry. In the US, folk is closely aligned to country music, which remains the most sought-after and lucrative music genre and, again, has a strong storytelling element.

European folk music tends to follow simple chord structures and melodies, so can offer a lovely introduction to singing. There are lots of local folk choirs and groups and they always have a welcoming and friendly atmosphere. Folk nights also often involve dancing, so can be a lot of fun!

POP

Pop singing is a relatively new style in the history of singing, and is in itself a very wide genre, spanning everything from rap (a near-spoken singing style) to rock (a very husky and throaty sound) and dance music (often sung in a more soulful style). It defies true definition. That said, pop vocal styles can broadly be defined by two things: rhythm and vocal placement.

The rhythm of pop songs tends to be 'syncopated'. That means the melody often falls just before or just after the beats. Pop songs are also often 'written' through the voice, so unlike a classical piece where the composer defines what the melody will be by writing it on a score, pop music songwriters often just 'come up' with a line. This can make the rhythms rather odd and complicated. An odd rhythm over a regular beat, to give the illusion of simplicity, is a hallmark of pop music

The use of the chest voice in the upper vocal register – also known as belting – is also prevalent in pop music. Both male and female pop vocalists are renowned for their ability to belt out high notes. This takes a huge amount of strength and skill, not to mention good technique and practice. So as much as we love to sing along to our favourite tunes in the car, be aware that pop is one of the more challenging styles for beginners, so start gently and don't push your voice until it's ready. Pop singers also use a lot of 'nasal twang', which is to say they use their noses to push out the sound (remember our nasal cavities are among our resonators – see page 48). Doing this can really help you get that quintessential pop sound.

All that said, if pop is really your thing, why not start with a pop choir? This can be a great introduction to singing in the style, as the choir leaders will arrange the songs to suit beginners' voices, so you can sing a Mariah Carey song without having to have her four-octave range. What could be better?

MUSICAL THEATRE

Musical theatre singing is generally a combination of classical, folk and pop. The songs tell a story, have relatively regular rhythms and usually have big and high vocal ranges, using a lot of 'belt' and 'twang'. There is also a lot of high articulation and drama: it's all about putting feeling and strength into a performance, and over-exaggerating everything.

Professional West End or Broadway singers train for years to be able to achieve the dramatic effects required – and belt out the high notes for two hours a day. They work hard on the 'mix' in their voice in order to smooth the break between their head and chest voices.

Local amateur dramatic clubs and community theatre productions are a great place to try out your musical theatre ambitions. Start tentatively by joining in the chorus pieces, which often won't even require an audition. Many choirs also put the musical theatre genre at the heart of their repertoires – a well-chosen chorus number performed by a large choir can be an amazingly powerful experience.

JAZZ

Jazz singers aim for a clearer and softer sound than pop and musical theatre artists. This is a more relaxed and enigmatic style, where belting and twang are less favoured than clarity and holding back a little.

Jazz as a genre tends to have a couple of distinctive elements. The first is it uses unusual chords and rhythms, playing heavily on the unexpected. Jazz musicians like things to sound a little strange, to create a bit of mystery, and this music is also often heavily improvised. There are basic structures and rhythms, but jazz singers have to be very skilled, especially in the transitions between notes, so they can move in different and unexpected ways each time they perform while still remaining in tune. Jazz does not always use words in songs: sounds like 'da' and 'bop' are used for improvising melodies. If you like to surprise and challenge an audience, jazz might be the genre for you.

SOUL OR GOSPEL

Soul and gospel singing are a little like pop singing, only they tend to have a religious or motivational message of inner strength. Soul and gospel singers use the chest voice and a lot of diaphragmatic support to make the belting voice really powerful. They also tend to use a lot of long notes in which they apply 'vibrato', meaning they whisk the sound so it seems as if it's waving or wavering. You can try vibrato yourself by singing two notes a semitone apart (say a C and a C#) over and over, then trying to speed up the transition so it sounds more like a shimmer.

Soul singers also tend to riff and improvise, slightly moving and redesigning the melody lines as they sing them, adding in additional slurred notes or changing the transitions between the notes. This takes a lot of skill, but can be achieved with practice. The technique provides an effective way of communicating passion and high emotion in a song, which suits the evangelical nature of gospel singing in particular.

BROADEN YOUR HORIZONS

Don't be afraid to widen out your tastes as you learn to sing. No doubt your teachers at school used to tell you that reading would help you to improve your writing – well, listening to different genres with an analytical ear will undoubtedly help you to find your own style and develop your voice. Try to balance your enjoyment of styles with thinking about which styles suit your voice best as you sing along: this will really help you to find both your range and your niche.

FIND A TEACHER

Whatever style of singing you want to pursue, and for whatever purpose, it's worth investing in a few singing lessons. Even one or two with a good teacher can give you a supportive and objective view of your voice that can help correct any learned bad habits, focus on individual things to work on and tailor exercises to your personal goals. Find a teacher who specialises in your chosen style and they'll be able to give specific advice. Best of all, a good singing teacher can work wonders for your confidence by providing lots of positive feedback to inspire you on your singing journey.

SING WITH OTHERS

Group singing is one of the most popular recreational activities in the world. In the UK alone, it is estimated that over two million people regularly sing in one of the country's 40,000 or so choirs. Over two thirds of these do not audition members, meaning you don't need to prove you have a 'good' voice in order to join, and you'll almost never have to sing on your own unless you choose to. This means it's far less scary than performing solo, but you can still get the buzz of hearing an audience applaud you!

The magic of choral singing has many dimensions. Combining many voices together makes everyone in the choir sound beautiful, even if some are less confident than others; the whole is far bigger than the sum of its parts. On a musical level, the group nature of a choir also allows for more than one note to be sung simultaneously (harmony), which can make choir performances a very powerful experience for audiences and choir members alike.

Learning harmonies in choir rehearsals can be somewhat challenging, especially to a beginner, but over time you will find it works wonders for your listening skills and your vocal confidence, as well as offering a sense of achievement and team work that is unlike any other. The shared activity of singing in harmony builds communities, helps overcome differences and creates deep friendships, even for the shyest among us.

THE SOLO SPOTLIGHT

Solo performing is an amazing way to grow your confidence, even if it seems daunting at first. As you feel yourself improve, why not give karaoke a go, or perhaps record and share a video of yourself? You could also try an open-mic night, which offers an accessible and supportive environment for soloists to hone their performance skills. Many open-mic nights will allow you to perform with a backing track, or you could find a friend with a guitar/keyboard who can accompany you and practise with you. If that all seems a little bit too much to begin with, you could volunteer for a short solo at choir where you can get the support and encouragement of the leader and your fellow singers, as well as taking on just a short section at a time rather than committing to a whole song.

People love to hear other people sing on their own, and most audiences will have a lot of respect for anyone that gives it a go. You can also gain a great deal of assurance from the feedback and compliments you receive from others (either in person or online). In venturing out into solo performance, just be prepared to invest the time in practising and also be ready for constructive feedback and suggestions from others, which will help you to improve. The more you perform on your own, the better you'll feel about it, but always remember that you do not need to be reliant on feedback to feel good about your singing. If you enjoy it, that's enough.

PEAK PERFORMANCE

You are ready to sing. You have learnt your song, you know the right techniques to apply, and you feel passionately about wanting to share your story. Just a few final considerations will put you on your way to giving a great performance, whether on your own or in a group.

- **Be relaxed in your body** – and don't be afraid to move around a bit while you're singing. Body language communicates so much alongside the voice, so using hand gestures, facial expressions and eye contact will help people – including you – connect with the emotions and messages of your song.

- **Conquer those nerves:** not an easy one, but the great thing about singing is that, because it's a form of controlling your breath, it can be extremely calming in itself. If you're a little nervous before a performance, do some deep breaths and exhale on a 'shh' sound for as long as possible. This also serves as a great singing warm-up. At the same time, remember that you are safe, nothing bad will happen, and you are singing for you. And the more you practise and perform, the more ready and confident you will be.

- **Dynamics:** varying the volume of your song – singing some parts more loudly and others more softly and quietly – will make your performance so much more emotive and interesting. Again, this helps connect us to the emotion of the song, since a song has an ebb and flow, embracing moments of climax and of reflection. Volume is the best way of communicating these peaks and troughs of emotion.

- **Enjoy it:** be clear in your message, move your mouth and be proud of what you're singing, so that the story has as much space as possible to echo and resonate with your audience. Enjoy yourself. Enjoy your moment. Smile.

JUST DO IT

At the beginning of this book I asked you to take a deep breath, open your mouth and sing. Since then, we've learned about the history, structure and purpose of the voice, as well as introducing lots of exercises to build strength and confidence in our singing ability. Hopefully I have also opened your mind to the many possibilities, opportunities and benefits that can await you as you travel on your singing journey.

In order to do something and to do it well, the first, most obvious step is to just do it. You've already taken that step. The rest is just practice, patience and pure enjoyment.

Nothing is more wholly of our minds, bodies, spirits and stories than singing. To communicate through the mysticism of the voice in all its beautiful complexity, and remarkable simplicity, is – I believe – one of humanity's greatest gifts. Singing tells our stories, it heals our souls, bonds us with others and helps us to find and communicate our place in the world. To use your voice is to be human and to be alive.

Let the world hear your voice. Take a deep breath, relax, and sing.

'If you're
gonna
sing,
sing loud.'

TRAVIS TRITT

QUOTES TAKEN FROM:

Clay Aiken is an American singer, television personality and actor. He rose to fame in 2003 when he came second place on *American Idol*.

Confucius was a Chinese philosopher, teacher and political figure.

Edith Piaf was a French singer and actress. Her trademark songs include 'Non, je ne regrette rien' and 'La Vie en rose'.

Esther Broner was a novelist, playwright and feminist writer.

Stephen Sondheim is an American composer and lyricist who known for a remarkable range of musicals including *West Side Story*, *Sweeney Todd* and *Into the Woods*.

Travis Tritt is an American country singer and songwriter.

BIBLIOGRAPHY

Abu-Lughod, L., 1999. *Veiled Sentiments: Honor and Poetry in a Bedouin Society*. Updated ed. Los Angeles: University of California Press.

Dunbar, R.: 2017 *Group size, vocal grooming and the origins of language*. Psychonomic Bulletin & Review 24:1 209-212.

Fancourt D & Perkins R (2018), *The effect of singing interventions on symptoms of postnatal depression: a three-arm randomised controlled trial, British Journal of Psychiatry*, 212, 119-121

Fancourt, D., Williamon, A., Carvalho, L., Steptoe, A., Dow, R. & Lewis, I. 2016. *Singing Modulates Mood, Stress, Cortisol, Cytokine and Neuropeptide Activity in Cancer Patients and Carers*. Ecancermedicalscience, 10(1), p. 631.

Feld, S., 2012. *Sound and Sentiment: Birds, Weeping, Poetics and Song in Kaluli Expression*. Durham & London: Duke University Press.

Monti, E., Aiello, R. & Carroll, L., 2016. *Singing: Some Do It for Passion, All Do It for Evolution*. Journal of Singing, 72(4), pp. 485-489.

Pearce E, Launay J, Dunbar RIM. 2015 *The ice-breaker effect: singing mediates fast social bonding*. R. Soc. open sci. 2: 150221.

Plancke, C., 2015. Shaping Affective Drives: An Anthropological Close-Up of Singing Subjects. Zeitschrift für Ethnologie, 140(1), pp. 91-109.

Reagon, C., Gale, N.S., Dow, R., Lewis, I., Van Deursen, R., 2017. Choir singing and health status in people affected by cancer. European Journal of Cancer Care, 26(5)

Richman, B., 1993. *On the Evolution of Speech: Singing as the Middle Term. Current Anthropology*, 34(5), pp. 721-722.

ABOUT THE AUTHOR

Rosie Dow is an experienced singer, choir leader and community musician, who has based her career on helping people discover the joy of singing. Her teaching focuses on fun and empowerment through singing, by using accessible breathing, vocal and confidence-building exercises to help people find their voice. As well as leading choirs directly, Rosie has worked with large networks of singing groups for people affected by cancer, and women in the military community, using singing as a way to offer support, fulfilment and friendship to people and communities facing challenges. Rosie has also worked with various prestigious universities to publish research on the social, biological and mental health benefits of singing, culminating in her completing an MA in Community Arts and Anthropology in 2018.

ACKNOWLEDGEMENTS

Thank you to Harriet Butt for being my inspiration to write this book. Harriet's support and encouragement has been invaluable throughout this process. Becoming an author has always been an ambition, but it would never have become a reality for me without her and the team at Quadrille. Thank you for making my dreams come true! Thanks also to Jessica and Emily for their amazing work on the designs.

I'd like to thank the members of my choir for being living proof that anyone can sing, and sing well, but also for the kindness and friendship they show to each other, and to me, week in, week out.

My mum has always been my musical inspiration, and singing has seen her through many difficult times. Every day she sings, and every week she finds new friends and experiences through singing. She and my dad have always been my number one fans and for that I am eternally grateful. Thank you also to my partner, Ian, for his constant support for all my endeavours, and his always-enthusiastic encouragement of me during the inevitably busy period of writing this book.

Finally, I would like to dedicate this book to everyone in the Tenovus Cancer Care Sing with Us choirs, who are the most fun, generous and inspiring people I have ever worked with. They have brought home to me the power of singing, in ways that changed my life forever.

Publishing Director Sarah Lavelle
Commissioning Editor Harriet Butt
Senior Designer Emily Lapworth
Illustrator Jessica Meyrick
Production Controller Sinead Hering
Head of Production Stephen Lang

Published in 2020 by Quadrille,
an imprint of Hardie Grant Publishing.

Quadrille
52–54 Southwark Street
London SE1 1UN
quadrille.com

Cataloguing in Publication Data: a catalogue record
for this book is available from the British Library.

ISBN: 978 1 78713 415 7

Printed in China